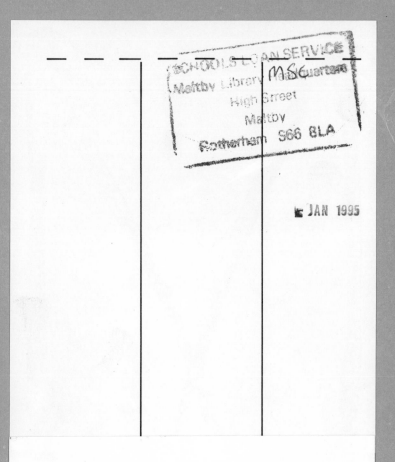

ROTHERHAM PUBLIC LIBRARIES

**This book must be returned by the date specified at the time of
issue as the Date Due for Return.**
**The loan may be extended (personally, by post or telephone) for
a further period, if the book is not required by another reader,
by quoting the above number   LM1 (C)**

WHO LIVED HERE?

My 1950s Home

KAREN BRYANT-MOLE

WATTS BOOKS
LONDON · NEW YORK · SYDNEY

© 1995 BryantMole Books

Published by
Watts Books
96 Leonard Street
London EC2A 4RH

Franklin Watts Australia
14 Mars Road
Lane Cove
NSW 2066

UK ISBN: 0 7496 2030 7
Dewey Decimal Classification Number: 941. 085

10 9 8 7 6 5 4 3 2 1

A CIP catalogue record for this book is available from the British Library.

Design and illustration: Chrissie Sloan
Photographer: Zul Mukhida

Consultant: Frank Jackson, Senior Lecturer
in History of Design, University of Brighton

Acknowledgements
The author and publisher would like to thank the Mudie family and
Mr and Mrs R. Shirley for their help with this book.
Photographs: The Advertising Archive 13 (bottom), 17 (top), 23 (both),
Beamish, The North of England Open Air Museum 4 (bottom), 6 (both), 7
(both), 10 (bottom), 13 (top), 15 (top), 17 (bottom), 19 (top), 21 (top), 25
(top), 27 (top), 29 (bottom); Bridgeman Art Library/Crown Estate/Institute
of Directors 4 (top)- We have not been able to locate the copyright
holder of the painting of Queen Elizabeth II by Denis Fildes, but if notified
we should be pleased to amend the acknowledgement in any future
edition; Chapel Studios 21 (bottom);
Robert Opie 5 (both), 15 (bottom), 19 (bottom), 25 (bottom),
27 (bottom), 29 (top).

Printed in Malaysia

Contents

Some of the more difficult words are explained on page 31.

The 1950s

When the 1950s began, George VI was king of Great Britain and Northern Ireland. He died in 1952 and his daughter, Princess Elizabeth, became queen. She was only 25 years old. Although people were saddened by the death of George VI, they were happy to have such a young and charming queen.

Coronation Day

Elizabeth was crowned as Queen Elizabeth II in 1953. The coronation took place on June 2nd at Westminster Abbey, in London. There were celebrations up and down the country on Coronation Day. Many people held street parties like the one you can see in this photograph.

Festival of Britain

In 1951 a great festival was held in London. It was called the Festival of Britain. Most people still remembered the difficult years of the 1940s when Great Britain fought in the Second World War. The Festival of Britain was seen as a time to look forward to a brighter future.

Rationing

Even though the war ended in 1945, there were still reminders of it in the 1950s. During the war, food, clothing and petrol were in short supply. People were given ration books with coupons. This meant that they could only buy a certain amount of these goods each week. Meat rationing continued until 1954.

1950s Houses

During the war, millions of houses were damaged or destroyed by bombs. Many people needed new homes. Lots of the men returning from the war got married and started new families. This added to the need for more homes.

Pre-fabs

The pre-fabricated house, or 'pre-fab', was a quick way of providing housing. Pre-fabs were made in sections that were fixed together. Thousands were put up during the late 1940s and early 1950s. Pre-fabs were only meant to last ten years, but some people are still living in pre-fabs today.

Council houses

Many new homes were built by local authorities. Local authorities are the organisations that run a town or area. Houses that are built and run by the local authority are called council houses. This is a picture of the 1000th council house to be built after the war by one local authority.

New Towns

Sometimes the best solution to the need for extra houses was to build whole new towns. These towns were built with a mixture of homes, shops, schools and places for people to work. This picture shows the building of a New Town called Peterlee.

Flat roofs

Flat-roofed buildings, like this house, became popular during the 1950s. The material the roofs were made from had to be replaced more often than the tiles on an ordinary roof. This house's square windows, plain walls and flat roof gave it a very 'boxy' look.

My Home

The house in this photograph was built in 1958. This is what it looks like today.

Plain windows, with large panes of glass, are known as picture windows.

The garage door and front door are new. They are made from stained, carved wood. When the house was first built, these doors would have been made from plain wood or metal that could have been painted in a colour such as yellow, green or red.

Very little else about the building has changed. What is different is the way in which it is furnished and decorated. For instance, there are now net curtains hanging up at most of the windows. When this house was first built, the owners would probably have hung up brightly coloured, patterned curtains. These would have been drawn to the sides to let in as much daylight as possible and give the rooms inside a light, airy feel.

Here are the family who now live in this house. They are the Mudie family. Michael is the youngest. He is standing in the middle. Behind him, you can see his elder brother, Johnny, and his mother, Lucy.

You will discover more about Michael, his family and their 1950s home as you read through this book.

The First Owners

The family who first lived in the house were called the Gadds. Mr and Mrs Gadd had three children. The children's names were Graham, Susan and Carol. When the family moved into their new home, Graham was 13 years old, Susan was 8 and Carol was 6. The Gadd family lived in an older, smaller house until they moved into their brand-new modern house in 1958.

This is a picture of a group of young soldiers. The photograph was taken at their training camp, just before they went off to join the Second World War. Mr Gadd was in the army during the war too. He was injured during a battle in France and was sent home to be looked after in an army hospital. There he met a nurse, called Moira. Mr Gadd and Moira were married in 1944. A year later, Graham was born.

These drawings show you the plan of the upstairs and downstairs of the Gadds' new home. You can look at the plan as you read the book. It will help you to work out where you are in the house.

Downstairs Plan

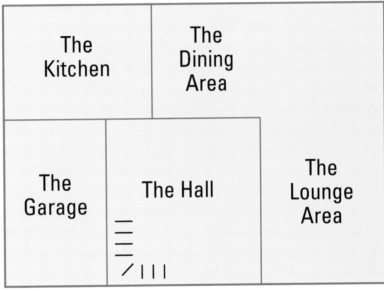

The Kitchen

The Dining Area

The Garage

The Hall

The Lounge Area

The Children's Room

The Bathroom

The Main Bedroom

Upstairs Plan

The Teenager's Bedroom

The Hall

This is what the Mudies' hall looks like now. Lucy sits at the desk under the stairs to write letters and make phonecalls.

Can you see the small table under the stairs? That was called a telephone table. There was a raised part for the telephone, with a shelf underneath for the phone books and a lower part that was used as a seat.

This is what the hall looked like when the Gadds moved into the house. The staircase is a type called an open tread staircase. That means that there are spaces between each of the steps. The Mudies have covered each step in carpet but in the 1950s it was fashionable to leave the steps as plain wood.

There are wooden banisters now. When the Gadds lived here the handrail and sides were made from wrought iron.

Open plan

A new idea that became popular during the 1950s was the 'open plan' house. Instead of having lots of separate rooms, the house had different areas. The house in this picture had no separate hall. The staircase came down into a general living area.

Telephones

Today, we take telephones for granted. In the 1950s, less than half the families in the country had a phone. To make a phone call to someone in another part of the country, the caller had to ring the operator and wait while the operator connected up the call.

The Lounge Area

When the Gadds moved in, they decided to buy modern furniture to go with their modern house. The thin, narrow legs that you can see were a feature of late 1950s furniture.

The seat near the window is called a couch. The word comes from the French word 'coucher', which means 'to sleep'. The back folded down to make a spare bed for visitors!

Look at the table. This 'kidney' shape was popular for both furniture and ornaments.

There is one big L-shaped living room. The Mudies use the longer part of the room as a lounge. They watch television in here and listen to CDs.

There was a tiled fireplace in the lounge. The Gadds were very lucky because their new home also had central heating. A coal-fired boiler heated up small radiators in all the rooms. Most homes in the fifties did not have central heating. The living rooms were heated by coal fires, electric fires or paraffin heaters. Bedrooms usually had no heating at all.

Television

At the beginning of the 1950s, very few families had a television set in their home. Instead, people listened to the radio. However, in 1953 there was a big increase in the number of families with television. This was because people wanted to watch the first ever televised coronation.

D-I-Y

People wanted their homes to look up-to-date. Do-it-yourself was the cheapest way to do this. It became a very popular hobby during the fifties. This do-it-yourself magazine even contained an article about how to make an electric washing machine!

The Dining Area

The dining area opens onto a new conservatory. The Mudies have a pine table and dresser.

The piece of furniture that you can see at the front of the picture is called a room divider. It was used as a way of breaking up the room into two different areas, without actually having a wall there.

Room dividers came in all shapes and sizes. Some went right from the floor to the ceiling, others stopped at waist height. Some were a mixture of cupboards and shelves, others were all shelves or all cupboards.

The wallpaper and carpet were both patterned. Geometric designs like these were popular in the fifties.

The Gadds had wooden furniture in their dining area, too. The long, narrow sideboard was used to store the best crockery and cutlery.

The light that hung over the dining table could be raised and lowered. It was known as a rise and fall light.

Entertaining

The lady in this picture is getting ready for a dinner party. Like the furniture, even the side lamp and the candle sticks had narrow legs.

There are dinner plates and side plates laid out on the table. The design on the plates was hand-painted.

Slums

Not everyone lived in new homes with modern furniture. There were still very many people living in terrible conditions. This family lived in one damp room. Homes like this were known as slums. As new homes were built, the slums were knocked down.

The Kitchen

Kitchen units really started to become popular in the 1950s. The kitchen in the Gadds' old house had two cupboards that didn't match, some shelves, a gas cooker, a ceramic sink and a wooden draining board. They were very proud of their new 'space-age' kitchen with its matching cupboards, and surfaces that were all at one height.

Can you see the electric kettle? Mrs Gadd had to remember to switch it off when the water boiled or the kettle boiled dry!

The sink in the Gadds' kitchen was made from stainless steel. In the 1950s stainless steel was quite a new idea. It became popular because it was so easy to care for and clean.

There was a Venetian blind at the window. Nowadays, the slats on Venetian blinds are often made from plastic, but in the fifties, they were usually made from metal.

The Mudies have a white, fitted kitchen. The hob and sink are set into the work surface. Michael likes watching breakfast television in the kitchen.

Washing machines

Most homes in the fifties did not have a washing machine. Those that did probably had a machine that was rolled to the kitchen sink on wheels. The machine had to be filled with water using a bucket or through a hose connected to a tap. This machine had a mangle, to squeeze as much water as possible from the clothes.

Fridges

Mrs Gadd was particularly pleased to have a fridge in her new kitchen. There had been no fridge in her old house. Food had to be kept cool in a cold cupboard, called a larder. Her new fridge kept food fresh for much longer than the larder.

The Main Bedroom

Lucy's bedroom is decorated in shades of pink and beige. The duvet, the stool and even the bedside lamp all fit in with this colour scheme.

The bedroom furniture had a walnut veneer. Veneer meant that thin strips of expensive wood, like walnut, were glued onto cheaper plywood. This made the furniture look expensive, without costing too much. The Gadds bought almost all their new furniture on H.P. (Hire Purchase). The Gadds paid back the money for the furniture week by week.

In the 1950s it was fashionable to decorate rooms in brightly-coloured, patterned materials. It was quite usual for the wallpaper, the carpet and the curtains to have completely different colours and patterns.

The sheets on the bed were made from nylon. Housewives liked these new nylon sheets because they were easy to wash and didn't have to be ironed.

1950s furniture

Most of the furniture in the Gadds' house was of a style that was common in the late 1950s. Furniture in the early fifties used to look very different. This picture was taken at a furniture exhibition in 1951. Can you see how much squarer the furniture looks?

Hair dryers

The hair dryer on the stool in Lucy's bedroom has a plastic casing. This 1950s hair dryer is made from an early type of plastic called bakelite. Bakelite was usually brown or black. Although bakelite was hard and strong, it was also brittle. This meant that it broke more easily than our modern plastics.

The Bathroom

The Gadds' bathroom had a bright blue suite. The bath was made from metal covered with enamel paint. Nowadays, baths are usually made from a type of plastic. Blue, green, primrose yellow, and deep pink were favourite colours for bathrooms in the 1950s.

Even though they brushed their teeth, all the Gadd children had fillings. Tooth decay in the fifties was much worse than it is today. Fluoride in our toothpaste helps prevent tooth decay.

There was a heated towel rail in the room. It used the same idea as a radiator. Hot water ran through the metal pipes. Towels were hung over the rails to dry out and warm up. The towel rail could be turned off by twisting the knob near the floor.

The curtains at the windows were made from a material called towelling.

The Mudies bathroom has a corner bath. The bathroom suite and tiles are all a pale peach colour.

Washbasins

1950s washbasins were often large and rectangular, like the one in this picture. You probably think that mixer taps and pop-up plugs are very modern, but this picture shows that they were available forty years ago.

Adverts

Adverts became an important way for manufacturers to get people to buy the things they made. This is a magazine advert for toothpaste. In 1955 adverts began to be shown on television, too.

The Children's Bedroom

Michael sleeps in this room. Last year the Mudies had a holiday in America. Michael brought back a baseball hat and glove.

Nowadays, the most popular wood for furniture is pine, but in the fifties, beech was more usual. Pine was thought of as a cheap wood and was often painted over. The girls' chest of drawers was made from pine. This sort of chest was known as a 'tallboy'. Each drawer front on this tallboy was painted in a different, bright colour.

Susan and Carol shared this bedroom. They had bunk beds. Each bed was covered with a patchwork bedspread. The bedspreads were made from colourful wool squares that were sewn together. The beds were made from a wood called beech. Furniture made from natural wood was very popular in the 1950s.

School

This is a picture of a 1950s classroom. The children have decorated it with Christmas decorations. Even though the picture was taken in December, the boy who is standing up is wearing shorts. Unlike today, boys under 12 usually wore shorts all year round.

Holidays

Every year, the Gadd family spent a week by the sea in Blackpool. The children in this picture are watching a Punch and Judy show on the beach. Most families in the fifties spent their summer holidays at British seaside resorts. It would have been unusual to go abroad.

The Teenager's Bedroom

Graham used his bedroom as a bed-sitting room. He had a chair, a tall lamp and a table in the room as well as the usual bedroom furniture. Notice the long, narrow legs on the lamp!

Graham liked to invite his friends up to his bedroom to listen to the latest records on his record player.

This is Johnny's room. Can you see the personal stereo on the bed? When he isn't listening to tapes, Johnny likes to play games on his computer.

The cover on his bed was a type called a candlewick bedspread. Candlewick bedspreads had small tufts of fluffy cotton that formed a lined pattern. They made the cover feel soft and warm. Underneath the bedspread there were sheets and blankets. Can you see Graham's slippers under the bed?

Teddy Boys

Many teenagers in the 1950s belonged to groups that dressed in a particular way. This boy was a Teddy Boy. Teddy Boys wore long jackets that looked a bit like the jackets from Edwardian times. 'Teddy' is another name for 'Edward'.

Teenagers

The idea of the 'teenager' first appeared in the fifties. There were clothes for teenagers and music for teenagers. Rock and Roll music began in the fifties. A type of music called skiffle was very popular too. Most teenagers enjoyed dancing. They usually had a live band, rather than records, playing at their dances.

The Garage

Lucy uses her car to drive the children to school, to go to work and to do the shopping.

The Gadds' car was a black Ford Popular. Instead of having flashing lights for indicators, a small, orange bar flipped up from in between the two side windows. At the beginning of the fifties almost all cars were black but by the end of the fifties, cars were available in a range of colours. Mr Gadd hoped to be able to afford a new, blue car soon.

Mr Gadd knew how to drive a car but Mrs Gadd didn't. Mr Gadd drove his car to work each day. Mrs Gadd walked the girls to school every morning and picked them up in the afternoon. Graham walked to school by himself. Mrs Gadd usually did the shopping at the local shops. If she wanted something special, she caught the bus into town.

Cars

The number of people who owned a car grew enormously during the 1950s. By the end of the fifties there were twice as many cars as there had been at the beginning. Before they owned a car, the family in this picture would probably have gone on their outing by train. As more and more people bought cars, the railways were used less and less.

American style

During much of the fifties, cars were squat and clumsy-looking. However, new ideas in car design came over from America. Some cars began to look much more stream-lined and had lots of shiny fittings made from a type of metal, called chrome.

Things to do

Patchwork

The bedspreads on the girls' beds were made from woollen squares. Patchwork can also be made from pieces of material, sewn together. Cut a piece of card into a square or a triangle. Draw around your template on scraps of old material. Cut out lots of identical pieces. Now stitch the pieces together. You could make a patchwork cushion cover.

Housing

Why not find out which of the houses in the area where you live were built in the 1950s? Your local authority's planning department should be able to point you in the right direction. You may even be able to see plans of the houses.

Make a plate

The patterns on the dinner service on page 17 were all hand-painted. Design your own fifties-style plate using a white paper plate and felt pens. You could base your pattern on some of the designs you have seen in the book or the design on the front cover.

Living history

Many of your relatives will be able to tell you about life in the 1950s. Some of you will probably have grandparents who got married in the fifties. You could ask them whether they still have any of the wedding presents they were given for their new home.

Glossary

bakelite	an early type of plastic
banisters	upright posts that support a stair's handrail
ceramic	made from a type of pottery
chrome	short for 'chromium', which is a bluish-grey metal
coronation	when a king or queen is crowned
couch	a piece of furniture that can be used as a bed
coupons	tickets which allow the holder to have or buy something
crockery	pottery plates, bowls, cups etc.
cutlery	knives, forks and spoons
design	pattern
enamel	a special sort of paint that does not crack when it gets hot
fluoride	a chemical which protects against tooth decay
geometric	made up of mathematical shapes
Hire Purchase	when an item is paid for in a number of stages
larder	a cool, walk-in cupboard, used for storing food
manufacturer	someone who makes something
nylon	a type of man-made fabric
operator	a person in a telephone exchange who connects up phone calls
organisation	a group of people who work together
paraffin	a type of oil that was used for heating
plywood	board made by gluing thin layers of wood together
rationing	only being allowed a fixed amount of something
stainless steel	a material made from a mixture of metals, including chromium
veneer	usually a thin outer layer of expensive wood
wrought iron	bars of iron, bent into decorative shapes

Index